Millionaires in Christ

Copyright © 2019 by Jeremiah M. Kapotwe.

ISBN Softcover 978-1-951469-68-9

All rights reserved. No part of this book may be reproduced or transmitted in any form or by any means, electronic or mechanical, including photocopying, recording, or by any information storage and retrieval system without express written permission from the author, except in the case of brief quotations embodied in critical reviews and certain other non-commercial uses permitted by copyright law.

Printed in the United States of America.

To order additional copies of this book, contact:
Bookwhip
1-855-339-3589
https://www.bookwhip.com

Contents

Dedication	iv
Acknowledgements	v
Foreword	vii
Introduction	1
1. THE POWER TO ACQUIRE WEALTH	6
2. THE COUNSEL OF THE WISE	14
3. ELEVATING YOUR SELF-CONCEPT, SELF-ESTEEM AND SELF-IMAGE	25
4. THE LAWS OF MONEY	38
5. MULTIPLE STREAMS OF INCOME	58
6. THE PRINCIPLES OF TIME MANAGEMENT	66
7. PRODUCER VERSUS CONSUMER	81
8. THE PRINCIPLES OF BUSINESS LEADERSHIP	91
9. GIVING BACK	105
CONCLUSION	116

DEDICATION

This book is dedicated to:

Severine and Miriam Kapotwe

Acknowledgements

My deepest gratitude to:

My wife for being a pillar of strength and supporting me in everything I do. You are the best.

Mr. and Mrs. Mwewa, your prayers have carried me in my life. May you be blessed beyond measure.

Victor, David and Bonke thank you for your support and for continuing to make a difference in people's lives.

Dr. Garnett, my Literary Advisor for assisting me to articulate my thoughts into a lucid, yet simple flow.

Deanne, for proofreading the manuscript and meeting the deadline.

My TOV family, you are the best people that keep me going even when I feel like giving up.

Rayolin Pillay, my business partner, you are a Godsend and a rare gem. Under your leadership the team is rock solid.

Mr. Kazenene Chilufya, your mentorship has paid off. You are indeed my hero and a role model to many.

Dr. M.S. Henry, a reservoir of wisdom and knowledge. You are truly my inspiration.

Dr. Paul Kariuki for our monthly coffee meetings and encouragement.

Eneya Banda, the loyalty and love you have shown to me and my family will forever be remembered.

To those that I have not mentioned due to space constraints, please know that I appreciate your support.

Foreword

The subject of wealth, money and all things material, has caused never-ending imbalance in the lives of many people. A somewhat pervasive, yet totally misguided tendency is that when some people arrive at a place of immense affluence, they become proud, aloof and even arrogant. On the other hand, most people spend their lives in a desperate quest to accumulate as much money as they can, simply for the equally misguided objective of living a self-centered, extravagant and ostentatious lifestyle.

Quite frankly, neither the arrogance that may accompany affluence, nor the accumulation of money for the sole and selfish aim of living a self-indulgent and self-absorbed life can be said to have the least basis in biblical wisdom. The sober truth is that God blesses us with any degree of financial independence for the purpose of being a source of blessing in the lives of others. Indeed, I totally endorse the view of Dr. Jeremiah M. Kapotwe, which is in perfect synchrony with biblical teaching, that God blesses us for the sole reason that He wants us to become a blessing in His kingdom.

In the nurturing hands of a true believer of the Word of God, worthily-acquired wealth is a tool to glorify the essence of God's inexhaustible abundance. I invite the reader to come to a sincere appreciation of the fact that the various laws and principles that Dr. Kapotwe enunciates so clearly and lucidly in this book are all based on timeless scripture. They should therefore be employed as a compass of sorts to guide one in one's own journey along the path of worthy income-earning ventures.

The greater responsibility, however, lies with the church. The church must not only strive to receive wealth, and encourage Christians to pursue financial independence through worthy and noble efforts, but also continue to improve on knowledge of the proper and profitable management of wealth, and impart this knowledge to their congregants.

The Bible is explicit in its encouragement that our best days are yet ahead of us. Dear reader, God's plan for your life is that you have joy and live life to the fullest. As it says in Jeremiah 29:11, "For I know the plans I have for you," declares the Lord, "plans to prosper you and not to harm you, plans to give you hope and a future." Our only obligation is to commit to using the wealth He blesses us with to unequivocally honor Him. To deploy our wealth to honor God means to take excellent care of our family, give to the poor; especially widows and orphans, and enhance the quality of our life.

Dr. Kapotwe is pre-eminently competent to teach us these basic principles. With the humility that is a hallmark of his personality, he comes to us with vast experience of all aspects of Christian ministry, and he is therefore well-equipped to address the issue of kingdom finance in this book. He deals exhaustively with the various aspects of finance, and its purpose in our lives. I do not mince words, neither do I exaggerate, when I declare that whatever nuggets of wisdom you glean from this book will deepen and strengthen your understanding of this all-important subject. Read this book to discover the truth about kingdom finance, for only the truth can set you free, so that you can come to God with equity, and with clean hands. As I remind you that only the truth from the Word of God can shift your life from poverty into abundant blessings, I leave you with these words from Acts of the Apostles 20:32, "Now I commit you to God and to the Word of His grace, which can build you up and give you an inheritance among all those who are sanctified." Amen.

Clive M. Gopaul
Senior Pastor
Conquering Through Prayer Ministries
P.O. Box 1153
Durban
4000
South Africa

Introduction

Looking at the events surrounding the Christian world today, I felt a deep conviction to write this book. The first question that assailed my consciousness was, "Does God want you to be wealthy?" Considering the title of this book, a more appropriate question might have been: "Does God want you to be a millionaire?" Yet, there is a subtle difference between the two questions. This is because, in real terms, one is a precursor to the other. You first have to be wealthy before you can become a millionaire. This might sound like a paradox, but it is not really. Wealth itself is a consciousness. It is the wealth consciousness that allows one to acquire material returns from worthy efforts. For the Christian, such consciousness will have to seek validation from another consciousness; the Christ consciousness.

Can anyone claim to be a complete repository of knowledge on what constitutes wealth consciousness? Probably not.

Given that the Holy Bible is the working tool for spiritual guidance in the affairs of the children of God, it should be our ultimate reference for the wellspring of wisdom that will see us through both the labyrinth of all that is relevant about Christ-centered wealth consciousness, and the ability to profit from worthy entrepreneurial effort. We know beyond an iota of doubt that the Bible contains a wealth of teachings on financial wisdom, which if properly and appropriately applied can't help but make one prosperous. Indeed, it would be appropriate to call this fountain of financial wisdom the foundational, biblical tenets for money management.

Theologians claim that there are more than 2 000 bible verses concerning money and its allied subjects. Why is the Word of God seemingly so fixated on money? Might it, in part be because money answers all things under the earth or that our financial lives can so totally consume us that money becomes an idol that relentlessly and mercilessly takes over our lives? Expressed differently, if we are not careful about how we view money, it can quite easily take God's place in our lives and lead us to a place of perdition.

This is why it is important that we gain authentic wisdom about the dynamics of Christ-centered wealth, to come to proper awareness of where to place our hope in matters of finance. That hope needs to be in Christ Jesus, and not in money.

The history of Christendom is full of examples of how people have allowed their money to enter into competition with God. The Bible states that you cannot serve God and Mammon. Christ-based financial wisdom becomes even more pertinent when we realize that money can easily lull us into a state of self-sufficiency that allows us to think that we don't really need God.

The global concept of self-made millionaires has slowly crept into the Christian circle undetected. The story is famously told of a millionaire who, in a fit of intoxicating conceitedness and vanity about his wealth, suddenly turned to an unfamiliar fellow guest at a dinner party, and righteously proclaimed, "I am a self-made man, you know. God has nothing to do with my millions!" The man he addressed this boast to simply gave him a look of sympathy, and calmly replied, "You need only one thing to make you really wealthy."
"What is that?" asked the millionaire.
"A little dose of humility!"

Tragically, once we begin to see money as the alpha and omega of our lives; descending into a willingness to do anything to get more of it, we are steadily but surely on the path to making money our master. In that case, what is wealth if not the slave of a wise man, yet master of a fool?

The truth is that a man's relationship with his money is two sides of a coin. On the one side, his money is his tyrannical master and on the other, it is his faithful servant. That is also why, as it is rightly said, it is contentment that made the poor man rich, and discontent that made the rich man poor. Truly, contentment doesn't come from having money or possessions, but from having a personal relationship with Christ. It is that personal relationship that is the foundation for the acquisition of authentic wealth.

In this book, you will come to comprehend that striving to deploy your talents, and your energy to generate wealth, and the heritage of enjoying the good that emanates from your labor, is an assignment that you must fully understand. The foregoing paragraphs dwelt on this assignment within the context of the power of wealth for good, and for evil. I also briefly touched on the need to consistently rely on God's wisdom.

This book will teach you how to properly manage your money for the optimization of your resources. Faith and determination, in combination with the right associations and attitude, divine creativity and an abiding gratitude for the love and guidance of God, will ultimately see you through.

Above all, you must be ready to feed your mind with the necessary information that you will need to become a millionaire in the truest context of the Christ consciousness. Welcome to that wisdom!

Dr. Jeremiah M Kapotwe
Durban, South Africa

CHAPTER 1

THE POWER TO ACQUIRE WEALTH

*Tapping into the
Creative Source of Affluence*

All wealth takes root from a source that can be termed the 'creative source of affluence'. I have a friend who is a gifted visual artist. I have been privileged to observe him at work, and am amazed at his creativity and scrupulous attention to detail as he produces spectacular portraits of men and women of influence, as well as world leaders. Should his creative expression come as a surprise? Most probably not. After all, the creative mind of God is the creative mind of man. God is the ultimate creator. If we agree that He created us in His own image, it is only logical to conclude that we are His co-creators. We need to embrace this creative side of our divine nature.

The Book of Genesis remains a constant source of fascination for me, if only because of its exhaustive recital of God's creative ability in bringing things into existence, beginning with the fundamental formlessness of matter itself.

"In the beginning God created the heavens and the earth. Now the earth was formless and empty, darkness was over the surface of the deep, and the Spirit of God was hovering over the waters." (Gen. 1: 1-2)

God's next great feat was to create us in His own image, and empower us with His creative ability.

"So God created mankind in his own image, in the image of God he created them; male and female he created them." (Gen. 1:27)

Is it even remotely possible to imagine that we can be created by such a powerful God, yet lack the same creative power as He possesses? Most definitely not, as this would be a contradiction of His nature. Your mind is fertile soil for the germination of creative seeds. The only thing required of you is to chisel away at this creative mind until it becomes a repository of the sheer creative genius of God, and the most fertile ground imaginable for the germination of the most divinely creative of seeds. God's creativity knows no bounds. It is infinitely free. His creativity has no rules.

Mortal genius is to do the common thing uncommonly well. Creative genius is to do the common thing with uncommon originality. Divine genius is to do the common thing with uncommon grace, and grace is something that we can access from God in all its abundance.

There is a certain sense of wonder when you are surrounded by wealth and power. Most wealthy people are creatively impulsive. They often act on a 'gut feeling', that indefinable, yet peculiarly strong feeling that continually propels them to open doors that were seemingly not there in the first place. As Christians, we need to be sensitive to that inescapable conviction that comes from the Holy Spirit that we should act in a certain way which will lead us to true wealth.

The ability to create is God's gift to humanity. It is the fatal combination of a lack of imagination, laziness and procrastination that kills mortal fortune. God expects His people to attain a state of immense wealth, and to live a life of sheer opulence and abundance.

Jesus said, *"I have come that you may have life, and that you may have it more abundantly."* (John 10:10)

The natural state that our Creator put in place for us is one of sheer opulence luxury. This is why His supply of abundance is magnificently inexhaustible. We are worthy of a limitless degree of material affluence as long as we acquire it honestly and through our best efforts. However, whether we have plenty of money, or just a little, we should strive to maintain the appropriate equilibrium.

Money can be a faithful servant, but it can also become a tyrannical master. We must always remember that we did not bring it with us at birth nor will we take it away when we make our inevitable exit from this earthly plane. This concept will recur throughout this book. We ought to always see money for what it is and nothing more. We should enjoy it, yet refuse to let it take over our life.

It is also imperative that we have an accurate understanding of the true nature of money. While it is said that money is the root of all evil, this is not entirely accurate. It is the love of money that is the root of all evil. Erroneous interpretation of this biblical concept is why most people make do with small rewards, shackled both by a self-righteous guilt complex about wealth, and the largely unarticulated belief that they are not worthy of the finer things in life. Furthermore, true wealth is access to what you need when you need it.

It is thus synonymous with authentic financial independence that enables you to indulge in the wonderful things that life can, and will offer, if, and when you achieve a state of substantial financial worth.

Our greatest possession on this earthly plane is freedom, and its fundamental source is material wealth. Paradoxically, after experiencing this freedom, the most significant feature of a man's last moments on earth is his arrival at the true freedom that is found in detachment. It is at this point that he can finally attend to the supreme will of his Creator, part of which is the requirement that we are generous with our wealth, as we are blessed so that we can be a blessing to those who are less fortunate than us. The other paradox is that, in being generous, and giving away that with which we have been blessed, we activate one of the most powerful mechanisms for generating even greater wealth.

The Power of Giving

Giving is the one of the best gifts given to humankind by our Heavenly Father. The principle of giving and receiving was founded by God from the beginning of time. For its sheer capacity to generate more of what it gives away, the act of giving has no match.

When you give with love, you unwittingly engage the universe in an exultant dance of economic advancement and monetary bliss.

On 16 May, 2009, the world woke up to the news that the two wealthiest men on earth, Mr. William Henry Gates III, Co-Founder of Microsoft, and Mr. Warren Edward Buffet, Chairman and CEO of The Berkshire Hathaway Group, had come together to found 'The Giving Pledge', an initiative through which they and other billionaires would pledge to give at least half their wealth to philanthropic causes across the globe. They would be joined a few years later by Mark Elliot Zuckerberg, Chairman and CEO of Facebook Inc., South Africa's Patrice Thlopie Motsepe, founder and Executive Chairman of African Rainbow Minerals and many others. As of October 2017, Gates was estimated by Forbes to be worth $90 billion; Buffet $86.3 billion, and Zuckerberg $74.2 billion. The more they gave, the wealthier they became. This does not come as a surprise. Giving is one of the most fascinating subjects in the annals of mankind. So much mystery has been woven around this issue that it is a discipline in its own right in the hallowed libraries of religious and mystic scholars. Rare is the adult who is not familiar with the oft-quoted saying: "The more you give, the more you will receive."

While few can unravel the mystery of the plenitude that accompanies generosity, it remains an incontrovertible truth that to give is to be at the receiving end of more of what was given away.

The act of giving is a very potent spiritual activity. It validates the very essence of compassion as one of our Creator's motives, and His vehicle for the display of love. Every act of giving should be an act of love. This is why it is backed by tremendous spiritual energy. Indeed, it is validly said that what you give will return to you in excess of what you gave. This is one of the most enduring secrets of genuine prosperity. Those who are profoundly aware of it have used it to advance their economic interests in remarkable proportions. It works to glorious benefit in the lives of both the rich and the poor. Truly, the more you give, with love, the more you will receive. It is an immutable law.

In the final analysis, the power to create wealth and affluence resides in the sublime fact that all things are created twice; first in the spiritual realm, and then later on the material plane. For centuries man has believed that the supreme secret to acquiring wealth is hidden somewhere, and is jealously guarded by the select few that manage to acquire riches on an extraordinary scale. Yet, the truth is that this secret is a secret, not because anyone is trying to keep it so, but because only a few people understand it.

This so-called secret is contained in a few simple words. *The human mind can accomplish whatever it believes it can achieve.* Truly wealthy people are visionaries. To be a visionary, one must be a dreamer. There are two types of dreamers, those that make no attempt to translate their dreams into reality, and people that comprehend and believe in the creative mind of the divine, and thus take concrete measures to fulfil their dreams. These are the dreamers who create something out of nothing, shaping our world for the better and creating untold wealth for themselves and for others.

CHAPTER 2

THE COUNSEL OF THE WISE

Wealth and Wisdom

One of the greatest paradoxes of wealth acquisition is that most of us are not even remotely aware that acquiring money also entails acquiring the requisite wisdom that guarantees both the accumulation and the sustenance of that money. Take, for example, the famous scenario of a monkey and a banana. Next time you have the privilege of being entertained by a monkey, try this experiment. Place two items before it: A banana, and a $100 bill. I can assure you that if it chooses the money instead of the banana, it is not a true monkey. True to its noble name, a monkey would dive straight for the banana.

The monkey will choose the banana, not because he is afflicted with a rare form of stupidity, but because he is blissfully ignorant of the fact that a hundred dollars can buy a whole lot of bananas. To put it differently, the monkey is grossly lacking in the wisdom of money. Most of us behave in a similar manner when presented with the choice between wisdom and money. Most would snap up the money without realizing that wisdom can buy them a lot of money.

"So that thou incline thine ear unto wisdom, and apply thine heart to understanding; Yea, if thou criest after knowledge, and liftest up thy voice for understanding; If thou seekest her as silver, and searchest for her as for hid treasures." (Proverbs 2:2-4)

When you pursue wisdom with all your heart, acquisition of money will be evidence of the success of your quest. Every search holds the possibility of finding something new. Every invention has been based on a search and research. In your quest for money, which is a perfectly valid aspiration, you need to be aware that two angels hover around you. One is the Angel of Wisdom, while the other is the Angel of Money. They both demand your unwavering attention, uncompromising devotion and unadulterated love. However, in your display of affection, you must be partial to the Angel of Wisdom. You must love her, and pursue her with single-minded focus and devotion.

When you do so, the Angel of Money will become insanely jealous, and will demand more attention.

"Wisdom is the principal thing; therefore get wisdom: and with all thy getting get understanding." (Proverbs 4:7)

The more you seek the Angel of Wisdom, the more the Angel of Money will seek you, following you wherever you go with blind devotion. This will lead you up the path of wealth, and into the wonderful world of financial freedom. This is the eternal and secret path to sustainable acquisition of money.

The Counsel of the Wise

But, where is this wisdom? It lies with the wise. Acquisition of wisdom begins with the acquisition of knowledge, as, in the final analysis, wisdom involves applying knowledge, and you cannot do so in isolation. Once you start to seek the knowledge of God for your life, one of the ways that God will communicate His knowledge to you is through other people. The Bible tells us that there is safety in the multitude of counselors, and that without appropriate counsel, our plans can go awry.

"A wise man is strong, yes a man of knowledge increases strength; for by wise counsel you will wage your own war, and in a multitude of counselors there is safety." (Proverbs 24:5)

"He who walks with wise men will be wise, but the companion of fools will be destroyed." (Proverbs 13:20)

That is why, once you truly start to seek the Wisdom of God, one of the first things He will do is to prune the negative people from your life that may hold you back. This is because your quest for sustainable wealth is incompatible with negative influences.

Superior Counsel

Have you ever invited a millionaire out for dinner? While this would seem most unusual, its utility actually lies in its novelty. Few people invite their mentors out. It's always the mentors who do the inviting.

One day, I invited one of my mentors for dinner at well-known restaurant in a beautiful suburb of Johannesburg, South Africa. To this day, that outing remains a life changing experience for me.

He looked into my eyes and said, "Son, if you want to be successful, you will need a tremendous amount of determination to see you through." I challenge you to have dinner with a millionaire that you admire, even if it costs you all your savings. I can guarantee a total transformation of your mind set. You will be surprised by the wisdom you gain from taking your mentor out to lunch or dinner.

Millionaires seem to have a subconscious urge to repay the favor by giving what they possess in excess, their wealth of financial wisdom. Indeed, it is a truism that no man is wise by himself. This is why anyone that aspires to any form of greatness must sit at the feet of another and tap his knowledge and wisdom. This is also true of those that aspire to genuine and sustainable wealth.

The Bible proclaims that no servant is greater than his master; nor can a messenger be greater than the one who sent him.

"Very truly I tell you, no servant is greater than his master, nor is a messenger greater than the one who sent him." (John 13:16)

After all, wisdom involves learning all one can learn, and then having the humility to realize that one does not know it all. He who teaches himself has a fool for a master and wise is he who humbly sits at the feet of someone more successful.

For, his superior wisdom will flow down to the pupil, as if propelled by some form of spiritual gravity. We must continue to partake of the fellowship of excellence that exists among the wise. For, is it not true that every student is someone's teacher; and every teacher someone's student? Socrates taught Plato; Plato taught Aristotle; and Aristotle taught Alexander the Great. To fly the way in which the eagle flies, one must perch on his back, and spread out the way he spreads his wings. Indeed, "when the pupil is ready, the master materializes!"

Examine Your Circle

Whose company are you keeping? No doubt, you are familiar with the popular saying, "Show me your friends and I will tell you who you are." While this quote is not credited to anyone in particular, and may have evolved over the centuries from folklore, Jim Rohn, the great American motivational speaker put it clearly when he said, "You are the average of the five people you spend the most time with."

The company you keep will play a huge role in how you turn out in many aspects of your life, money making being one of the most significant. If you relate to people who are obviously drifting in life, and have no drive whatsoever, you stand a very good chance of developing these traits.

On the other hand, if you associate with successful people, there is a high chance that you will be successful in life. If you associate with millionaires, you stand a higher chance of becoming a millionaire yourself. This is because great minds possess great habits. They carefully select their partners, and stepping into their world could make a significant difference in yours. Listen to them speak. Listen to their tapes. Read their books. Make friends with them. Do all these things so that you can move towards their own form of greatness. Ordain yourself in the circle of the spiritual. Invite yourself into the circle of the influential. Declare yourself a member of the millionaires' club. Admit yourself into the clique of intellectuals. Become a member of the Millionaires' Club.

Spend Time with The Right People

It is true that we become like the people we spend time with, and the degree to which we are successful in life depends on who we associate with. Choose your associates wisely. It doesn't matter how smart and talented you are, what skills you possess, where you are born, or which family you come from. All other factors considered, the people you surround yourself with will determine how successful you will be in life. Do not cling to relationships with people who are not adding value to your life.

I was fortunate to learn this early in life and I have been able to narrow my circle down to people who have the focus and determination that serve as motivators for me. Indeed, their positive impact is pushing me higher and onto the next level every day.

"Can two walk together, unless they are agreed?" (Amos 3:3)

The company you keep goes a long way in determining who you are likely to become. If you keep the wrong company, you are likely to miss great opportunities for progress. The cliché that says, "Your network determines your net worth in life" is very true. If you have great minds in your network, the ideas that come up from your conversations could lead to new concepts and possibilities, which might not occur with the wrong set of people. In the words of Eleanor Roosevelt, "Lesser minds discuss about people, average minds discuss people but great minds discuss about ideas."

The Circle of Winners

The saying, "show me your friends, and I will tell you who you are" makes sense because only those who have been able to achieve success and greatness can properly mentor impressionable minds.

That is why surrounding yourself with winners will make you a winner. On the other hand, surrounding yourself with losers will make you a loser. Never underestimate the power of influence in your life. This is not an instant process, but a gradual accumulation. Given time, you find yourself taking on the character of the people you are exposed to on a daily basis. Irving Himmel wrote, "No one has ever made himself great by showing how small someone else is." Only great minds will tell that you, too, can do it. Lesser minds will tell you that you can't. According to Henry Ford, "Your best friend is the one who brings out the best in you."

Your Time

Who do you spend your time with? How do you spend your time? Your time is your most valuable asset. When you give someone time, you give him a piece of your life that you will never recover. The Bible notes the importance of

"redeeming the time, because the days are evil." (Ephesians 5:16)

You can lose your money, opportunities, health, job and more, yet recover them. However, if you fritter away your time, you can never recover it. When you relate to someone, is the association of benefit to you? Does he share your vision?

Is your association helping you to move to the next stage of your life? A good network of alliances can be life changing.

To figure out whether the people you associate with are a positive influence, you have to be fully aware of your mission, vision and goals. Once you know what these are, you need alliances that truly work for you. Whenever you are relating to a group of people, you should ask yourself three questions. The first is: Am I in the right place? The amount of time you spend with people shows the value you attach to the association. Life is too short to experiment with things that add no value to your life. Always evaluate what you spend your precious time on, including your leisure hours and productive times. The second question is: Are these people's objectives congruent with mine? Thirdly, what are these people doing for me? If they are helping you to grow by giving you challenging opportunities, you are probably in the right place. Your alliances determine what you will be reading, and what tapes and videos you will be listening to. To a large extent, they dictate what you will be doing, thinking, and feeling. They also determine what you will be talking about and where you will be in the near future, all things being equal.

When all is said and done, as the famous saying goes, "No man can exist as an Island unto himself." Every advance, and every demotion in life comes about through our fellow human beings, in one way or another. We can stack the odds in our favor by carefully selecting those whose company we keep on a constant basis, if only for the simple reason that he who walks with the wise will grow wise.

CHAPTER 3

ELEVATING YOUR SELF-CONCEPT, SELF-ESTEEM AND SELF-IMAGE

The Supreme Secret

For millennia, man has entertained the belief that the supreme secret of success is hidden somewhere. Furthermore, man believes that this secret has been jealously guarded by the select few who manage to achieve extraordinary success. I have a piece of liberating news for you. There may well be a supreme secret of success, but this is not a secret because anyone is trying to keep it that way. It is a secret for the rather prosaic reason that only a few understand it. And what is this secret? It is contained in ten simple words. *"The human mind can accomplish whatever it believes it can!"* It lurks quietly in the Bible:

"Whatever you ask for in prayer, believe that you have received it, and it will be yours." (Mark 11:24)

Scottish thinker and writer, Eileen Caddy highlighted the power of the word, 'believe'. On an early morning stroll on the picturesque cliffs of Dover in South East England, she penned the words, *"The secret of making something work in your life is, first of all, the deep desire to make it work, then the belief that it can work, then to hold that clear, definite vision in your consciousness and see it working out."* Your rock-solid, deep-seated belief will fuel your vision; if you do not have the conviction that your mission will see the light of day, how can you justify your lofty vision? But, before your belief can become deep-seated, you must believe in GOD, and in yourself, and before you can truly believe in yourself, you must have healthy self-esteem.

Self-Concept and Self-Esteem

Self-concept is what you understand about yourself. It takes into account your social character, abilities and thought processes. Self-concept is best defined as a combination of *self-image, self-esteem* and your *ideal self*. To break these down simply, your self-image is how you see yourself, your self-esteem is how much you value yourself and your ideal self is the vision you have for yourself; in other words, how you wish you could be.

Your self-concept is formed when all these are taken into account. However, it is important to note that your self-concept does not always coincide with reality. In fact, more often than not, the way we view ourselves is distorted and unrealistic. We are often overly critical of ourselves and our abilities. This is where self-awareness comes into the picture as it enables us to be aware of what is true about ourselves.

"For you created my inmost being; you knit me together in my mother's womb. I praise you because I am fearfully and wonderfully made; your works are wonderful, I know that full well." (Psalms 139:13-14)

This is important to believe that you are fearfully and wonderfully made in the image of God. You probably understand that your view of yourself is true, while others may see you quite differently. Therefore, awareness is the process of moving your view closer to the truth. When all is said and done, your journey to financial success begins with a healthy self-concept. The only way to achieve this is to invest heavily in yourself, and in your mind.

Invest in Yourself

Investing in yourself yields one of the best possible returns on investment. Whether it is learning a new skill, developing yourself personally or professionally, tapping into your creativity or hiring a coach, you need to give to yourself first before you can give to others. The money you wish to make is in the pockets of other people. To access it, you must offer them some form of service. Therefore, you should take responsibility to develop your gifts and talents, so that you can best serve others. Investing in yourself is a manifestation of self-love that nurtures a healthy self-concept.

How to Invest in Yourself

1. *Set goals.* Learn how to set realistic, time-specific personal and business goals for yourself. Not taking the time to set worthy goals, is like driving in the dark with the headlights turned off. You will not know where you are going, and you will waste precious time. My college professor used to emphasize that one's goals must be S.M.A.R.T: Specific, Measurable, Attainable, Relevant and Timely.

2. *Honor your intuition.* Learn to trust your 'gut instincts' and honor the message that they send. Listening to your intuition will enable you to make better decisions.

Valuing your intuition by not allowing others' thoughts, feelings or statements to detract you from what you know to be authentic, is very empowering. Paying attention to how you feel will help you make better, smarter and quicker decisions.

3. *Invest time in your creativity.* Creativity should galvanize us towards continual learning and lifelong activity. It enables us to be inspired, and appreciate the beauty in our world. The creative nature of Man is the creative nature of God, and to tap into His creative nature, we must take on, and assume His nature.

4. *Invest in building your confidence.* People who know their value always have something to say that others will listen to. Invest in yourself by developing an understanding of your value and what you can offer others. Learn to have the courage to speak your truth. The more you love yourself and own the value that you offer, the more confident you will become in sharing it with others.

5. *Read educational books.* Books and audio books are a great resource for building knowledge and expertise in any area. Knowledge is unlimited. You need to drink from the fountain of knowledge on a daily basis in order to be a better person, and to make a meaningful contribution to society.

6. *Attend seminars and workshops.* This is important to expand your knowledge and skills in your business and personal life. It is also an opportunity to meet and interact with like-minded people. More money is made by forging quality relationships that are outside our usual circle of influence. Networking is one of the keys to achieving your financial goals. Friends have a tendency to support one another.

7. *Take care of your health.* The best way to achieve this is by eating well. Eat correctly each day, fueling your body with essential nutrients. Organic and healthy food will make you feel better and you will have more energy.

Exercise daily. My first day at the gym was almost my last day there. I wanted to quit because I was out of breath, became extremely dizzy, and felt like throwing up. However, I persevered, and regular exercise has thankfully become an inalienable part of my daily routine. Exercise gives you the energy to take on the day with confidence because of how it makes you look and feel.

8. *Choose to be happy.* Happiness is a choice. Happy people tend to focus on the positive aspects of life, rather than the negative. They are not held hostage by their circumstances. They are always looking for reasons to be grateful.

Since you have only one shot at life, choose to be happy, despite your circumstances. A bad day does not equate to a bad life. Keep moving forward, in the grateful knowledge that every day is a gift from God.

9. *Continually work on your 'Big List'* of everything you want to achieve, do, see, feel and experience in your lifetime. After all, what is the point of becoming a millionaire if you haven't the faintest clue what you ultimately wish to do with your millions? Your list may be ongoing, but you can start by listing 100 things. Each month or so, make sure you cross off at least one of the items.

10. *Invest in a mentor, or coach.* This is the person who can assist you to put all the above strategies into action. A coach is your partner in success. It is his job to help you to create and implement your plan, so you can become the best that you can be.

When you richly invest in yourself, a world of otherwise unseen opportunities opens up. If you have a business where you sell your services, you should know that no one will invest in you until you invest in yourself. Investing in yourself emotionally, physically, spiritually and financially will enable you to become the best version of yourself. Your self-concept and self-esteem will grow and you will become a magnet for other people.

Become the Best in Your Field

"Whatever your hand finds to do, do it with your might; for there is no work or device or knowledge or wisdom in the grave where you are going." (Ecclesiastes 9:10)

In truth, there is really no such thing as being born into success. Rather, entrepreneurs who lead the pack in their field, and have an extraordinary intuitive feel for their specialty, tend to have an unyielding focus and work ethic. Usually, it is not a question of some natural talent or brilliance that they possess. Instead, they have achieved an unassailable level of experience and practice. Here are a few suggestions on how you can strive to be the best in your area of specialization.

1. *Focus on a field that you have passion for.* Highly successful people are emotionally and personally engaged in their work, on a level beyond intellectual curiosity. Their personal commitment motivates them to put in the long hours and sustain the fervent curiosity to master their field.

2. *Learn by doing.* An entrepreneur makes something out of something else. The best way to become an entrepreneur is to build businesses. Henry Ford's first two automobile companies failed miserably. Sometimes, one should psychologically desire failure because that is how one learns.

If you are not going to start your own business, at least work in as small a company as possible to learn as many skills as possible.

3. *Find a mentor.* When selecting a mentor, look for somebody who is already doing what you see yourself doing in five to ten years' time. A healthy mentorship relationship is like that between a parent and a child. A good mentor should be older than you and at a point in his career that he wants to give back. Personality is also important. Your mentor's spirit should match yours.

Dream Big Dreams

Only dream big dreams, believe in them and commit to, not just dreaming the dream but living it. Usually, the bigger the dream, the bigger the effort, as small dreams can only inspire weak effort. It takes sixteen hours to assemble a Toyota and sixteen weeks to handcraft a Rolls-Royce to the customer's exact specifications.

Ask the average millionaire, and he will tell you that if he had to attribute his phenomenal success to one thing, it is that he steadfastly believed in his dreams, even when no one else did.

Go the Extra Mile

Most of the world's millionaires are truly outstanding people. Outstanding individuals go the 'Extra Mile' in all they do. Doing more than is required calls for personal commitment and discipline without outside forces compelling you to do something.

"If anyone forces you to go one mile, go with them two miles." (Matthew 5:41)

Going the extra mile differentiates the super business person from one who spends his life following the super business person. Go the extra mile in order to be counted as an industrious person.

Attitude is another major difference between high achievers and the not-so-successful. Poor performing people who believe that they are short changed and cheated are more likely to ask, "What's in it for me?" In contrast, from the start of their careers, high achievers seek every available opportunity to exceed expectations. They are prepared to go the extra mile and work hard.

Why does 'going the extra mile' make such a huge difference in the eventual outcome of our lives? The reason is simple. The 'Extra Mile' is a lonely and desolate stretch that few are willing to endure.

Yet, the lone person on this lonely stretch stands out and is immediately visible when opportunity comes calling. While such people are regarded as 'lucky', in reality, what they have done is make themselves available. An ancient law of nature states that what we commonly refer to as 'luck' is nothing more than the meeting point of *'preparation'* and *'opportunity'*. In truth, when opportunity comes knocking at the door of the prepared person, a 'lucky' man is born!

But, what is this extra mile? It is what you do after you have done that which you were expected to do. When you do more than you are paid to do, you will eventually be paid more for what you do. Always look for the slightest opportunity to exceed expectations and you will reap financial reward and high esteem from your employer and customer.

Stamp Your Service with Your Trademark of Excellence

To become a roaring financial success, you must ensure a fine finish to your product or service. Commit to increasing your value at work. Rather than having a job, let your work have you.

Let your job have such a tight hold of you that, wherever you are, it has you for keeps. Let your job have you when you retire to bed at night.

When you awaken in the morning, your work should be sitting at the foot of your bed, saying, "Get up! It's time to come to me!" When your work arrests you totally, you will amount to something.

Think of quality rather than quantity. If you do just one thing absolutely right, it will educate you more, improve you much more, and give you more satisfaction, than doing a thousand poor jobs.

The quality you bring to your work will bring your character to the same level. The habit of doing things to a perfect finish will strengthen your character. How can you respect yourself when you constantly slip up in your work? When you lose your self-respect, won't you also lose your self-confidence?

Finally, when you lose both self-confidence and self-respect, you will definitely lose your self-esteem. Make self-respect and self-confidence your stepping stones on your road to excellence. Your contract with yourself means that you have to offer your best. Will you not hold yourself in higher esteem if you have the approval of your conscience? Sew character and individuality into the fabric of your work, so that anyone who comes across he will see nothing but your trademark of excellence. Your reputation is your capital. Henceforth, do away with "fairly good", "pretty good", and "good enough!" There is no room for incompetence in this glorious age of opportunity.

Wherein lies the excuse for being second class in an age when first class is in serious demand? The best substitute for genius is your 'Trademark of Excellence', which is a greater capital than cash.

CHAPTER 4

THE LAWS OF MONEY

Each of us has the inalienable right to aspire to become a millionaire, as genuine financial independence, that point at which one need not ever worry about money again, is crucial to living a life of peace. Fortunately, financial independence is easier to achieve today than it ever was. In fact, this being the Golden Age of mankind, wealth surrounds us on every side. Make no mistake, money is a spirit in its own right. It possesses its own energy, and because of this, it is largely attracted to people who understand it's utility, purpose and essence, and treat it well.

"A feast is made for laughter, wine makes life merry, and money is the answer for everything." (Ecclesiastes 10:19)

Money answers all things in this world. Learning the skill of wise deployment of money is of the utmost importance. That is also why money tends to find its way to those who can deploy it productively for the production of valuable goods and services, and invest it to create opportunities and wealth for others. By the same immutable token, money flees from those who abuse it, treat it poorly, or spend it in non-productive ways.

It is your moral obligation to acquire as much money as you honestly can, and worthily employ it to enhance the quality of your life and that of others. There are nineteen laws of money that you need to familiarize yourself with.

1. *The Law of Cause and Effect*

Everything happens for a reason. That means there is a cause of every effect. It also means that we live in a world governed by law, not by chance. Everything happens for a reason; whether or not we know that reason.

Success or failure; wealth or poverty, all have specific causes. Every action has an effect or consequence of some kind or another, whether or not it is obvious, and whether we like it or not.

Since this law recognizes that all prosperity and success is the result of specific actions, if you are clear on the result you want, you can achieve it by studying others who have accomplished the same goal, and doing exactly what they did.

Expressed simply, you can acquire whatever money you want if you do what others have done before you to achieve the same results. If you don't, you won't. It is as simple as that. The most important principle of business is that you become what you think about most of the time.

Specifically, the way you think about money and about your financial situation largely determines your financial circumstances today.

2. *The Law of Belief*

Whatever you truly believe with feeling, will become your reality. That means that you will always act in a manner consistent with your beliefs about yourself. You don't necessarily believe what you see. Rather, you see what you already believe. You tend to reject information that contradicts what you have already decided to believe, whether those beliefs are based on fact or fantasy. This premise is particularly valid with regard to money.

The best belief pattern you could possibly adopt is that you are destined to be a millionaire. When you are absolutely convinced of this, you will engage in behaviors that make it a reality. Avoid self-limiting beliefs. No one is better than you. No one is smarter than you are. If someone else is achieving more, it is because he has developed his natural talents and abilities more than you have.

3. *The Law of Expectations*

What you confidently expect, will inevitably become a self-fulfilling prophecy. The pronouncements you make about your life render you your own fortune-teller. The more you confidently expect good things to happen to you, the more they will.

"For we walk by faith, not by sight." (2 Corinthians 5:7)

If you expect something negative to happen, you are usually not disappointed. Wealthy people expect to be rich. Your expectations are largely under your own control.

Simply expect the best for yourself. Imagine that you can accomplish anything that you put your mind to. Believe that whatever you have accomplished up to now is a mere fraction of what you are truly capable of. Walk by faith.

4. The Law of Attraction

You are a human magnet. You attract people and circumstances that are in harmony with your predominant thought pattern.

This is a particularly powerful law that goes a long way in explaining success and failure in business and personal life. It states that you have attracted to yourself everything you have in your life because of the way you think. You can change your life by changing the way you think. When you develop a burning desire for wealth, and think about it all the time, you generate a force field of positive emotional energy that attracts people, ideas and opportunities to help you turn your goals into realities.

5. The Law of Correspondence

Your outer world is not only a reflection of your inner world, but it also corresponds with your dominant pattern of thought. This means that all that happens to you in the long term corresponds to something inside of you. Therefore, if you want to improve anything in your life, start by changing the inner aspects of your mind. This is referred to as your 'mental equivalent'.

Create within yourself the mental equivalent of what you want to experience on the outside. You cannot achieve it on the outside until you have first created it on the inside.

6. *The Law of Abundance*

Our universe is lavishly abundant. There is sufficient money for all who truly desire it, and are willing to subscribe to the laws governing its acquisition.

We live in a generous universe and are surrounded on all sides by opportunities to acquire all we truly and worthily desire.

Your attitude to money will determine whether or not you become rich. People become wealthy because they decide to do so, and because they believe they have the ability to fulfil their objective. They therefore, consistently do things that turn their beliefs into realities.

Conversely, people are poor because they have not yet decided to become rich. Ask yourself a simple question. "Why am I not already rich?" Whatever your excuses may be, get rid of them. Thousands of people have had far greater obstacles to surmount, yet they become financially successful. So can you.

7. The Law of Exchange

Money is simply a medium of exchange. People exchange their labor in the production of goods and services for the goods and services of others. In the ancient world, this exchange did not involve money.

Money has made this process more efficient. Today, we exchange our work for money, which we then use to purchase the results of the work of others. Invariably, money is a measure of the value that people place on goods and services. What a person is prepared to pay determines the value of something. Furthermore, the amount of money you earn is a measure of the value that others place on your contribution.

You are paid in direct proportion to three factors: the work you do, how well you do it, and the difficulty of replacing you. It follows that, to increase your earnings, you need to increase the value of the work that you put in. This could include one, some, or all of the following: upgrade your knowledge or skills; improve your work habits; work longer and harder; or work more creatively. The highest paid people are those who are continually improving in one or more of these areas to add greater value to the work they deliver.

8. *The Law of Capital*

Your ability to work is your most valuable asset. If you apply your earning ability to the production of valuable goods and services, you will generate wealth. What you earn is a direct measure of the extent to which you have developed your earning ability. In applying that ability, your most precious resource is your time. How much time you put in largely determines your income. Time and money are interchangeable. If you spend them, they are gone forever. On the other hand, you can invest them, and obtain recurrent returns, even for perpetuity. Better still, you can invest your time or money in becoming more knowledgeable and skilled to increase your value. A smart strategy is to invest a percentage of your income in personal and professional development.

9. *The Law of Time Perspective*

The most successful people are those who take the longest time period into consideration when making current decisions. Top performers tend to make decisions and sacrifices that may not pay off for many years, sometimes not even in their lifetime. Such people are willing to pay the price of success for a protracted length of time before they achieve it.

They think about the consequences of their financial decisions in terms of what they might mean in five, ten, fifteen and even twenty years down the line.

Your financial ascent commences the day you begin to act in terms of the possible long-term consequences of your actions. Longer term organization of your financial life and priorities in alignment with your future goals and ambitions tends to improve the quality of your decisions, while your life starts to get improve almost immediately.

Delayed gratification is key to financial success. Learn to practice self-mastery, self-control and self-denial. Learn to sacrifice in the short term so that you can savor greater rewards in the long term. That is why self-discipline is the most vital personal quality for long-term success. It is the ability to make yourself do what you should do, when you should do it, whether or not you feel like it. Ultimately, sacrifice in the short-term is the price you pay for security in the long-term.

10. *The Law of Saving*

The person who saves 10% or more of his income throughout his lifetime earns financial freedom in the long run. Develop the habit of saving part of your salary. Today's savings guarantee the security and the possibilities of tomorrow.

Pay yourself first. Begin to save 10% of your income, and never touch it. This is the seed for long-term financial accumulation. Do not use it for any other reason other than to assure your financial future. You will soon become accustomed to saving 10%, giving another 10% to your local assembly and living on the remaining 80%.

We are creatures of habit. When you save on a regular basis, it becomes habit. Many millionaires start by saving 10%, and graduate to 20%, and even more.

11. *The Law of Conservation*

Your financial future is not determined by how much you make, but by how much you keep. You may make a lot of money in the course of your working life and could even enjoy sporadic windfalls. However, the true index of how well you are doing is how much you are able to keep.

Authentic millionaires are fastidious about putting away chunks of money on a regular basis, ensuring that they have reserves set aside for an economic downturn. Calculate your current true net worth. Value all your assets at current potential returns on sale if you had to convert them into cash quickly. Add up all your bills and credit card balances, and then subtract them from your assets to obtain your current net worth.

Now, divide your net worth by the number of years you have been working. The result is the net amount you have actually earned each year after the cost of living. Is the figure to your satisfaction? If not, start to do something about it today.

Parkinson's Law states that expenses rise to meet income. This is one of the most important laws of money and wealth accumulation and is why most people enter their twilight years in poverty. No matter how much money people earn, they tend to spend the entire amount and a little bit more besides. There never seems to be enough.

Financial independence comes from violating Parkinson's Law. Only when you summon sufficient willpower to resist the powerful urge to spend all you earn will you begin to accumulate money and move ahead of the crowd. As a corollary, when you ensure that your expenses increase at a slower pace than your income, you can save or invest the difference and become financially independent.

From today, resolve to save and invest 50% of any increase in your income. This still leaves you the other 50% to do with as you wish. Learn to live on that.

12. The Triad Law

Financial freedom is a stool with three legs: Savings, Insurance and Investment.

You owe it to your loved ones and yourself to build a financial fortress over time. Your estate should ensure immunity from financial insecurity. To achieve this, you need to maintain the correct proportions of your finances in savings, insurance and investment.

The first vital step is to protect yourself against the unexpected by ensuring that your liquid savings equal six months of normal expenses. This means that if you lose your source of income for up to six months, you have sufficient savings to tide you over. The very act of saving this money and putting it into a high-yield savings or money market account, will give you enormous confidence and peace of mind.

The second step is to have adequate insurance for emergencies that you cannot pay for out of your bank account. Have sufficient health insurance to provide for yourself and your loved ones in a medical emergency. Insure your car. Insure your life so that, should you die, those who depend on you will be well provided for.

The third vital step is to accumulate capital until your investments are paying you more than you earn.

13. *The Law of Investing*

Investigate before you invest. Do not be rushed into parting with money. Painstakingly investigate every aspect of an investment before you make a commitment. Demand complete, honest and accurate information. If you entertain any doubts or misgivings, keep your money in the bank or in a money market investment account rather than risk losing it.

A Japanese proverb goes, "Making money is like digging with a nail, while losing money is like pouring water on the sand." The only thing easy about money is losing it. Simply refuse to lose money. If there is a possibility that you will, don't part with it in the first place. Also, remember the saying, "When a man with experience meets a man with money, the man with the money is going to end up with the experience and the man with the experience is going to end up with the money." A fool is soon parted from his money. Be careful.

Only invest with experts who have a proven successful track record with their own money. Invest only in what you fully understand and believe in.

Take investment advice only from those who have demonstrated successful outcomes from offering themselves such advice.

14. *The Law of Compound Interest*

If you invest your money carefully, and allow it to grow at compound interest, you will eventually become rich. Compound interest is one of the miracles of economics. Albert Einstein described it as the most powerful force in the world.

When money accumulates at compound interest over a long enough period of time, it increases more than you can imagine. You can use the Rule of 72 to determine how long it would take for your money to double at any rate of interest. You simply divide the number 72 by the interest rate. For example, if you were receiving 8% interest on your investment, and you divided the number 72 by 8, you would get 9. This means that it would take you nine years to double your money at 8% interest.

The key to compound interest is to put the money away and never touch it. Once you start accumulating money and it begins to grow, do not spend it for any reason. If you do, you lose the power of compound interest, and even if you only spend a small amount today, you will be giving up what could be an enormous amount later on.

Begin a regular, monthly investment account and commit yourself to investing a fixed amount for the next five, ten or even twenty years. Select a company with a family of mutual funds and investment instruments, and keep your money working, month after month, year after year.

15. The Law of Accumulation

Any substantial monetary fortune is merely the cumulative sum of multiple little efforts and sacrifices. The process of accumulation demands discipline and persistence. Initially, you will see very little difference, but gradually, your efforts will begin to bear fruit, and you will begin to pull ahead of your peers. Your finances will improve and your debt will disappear. Your bank account will grow and your whole life will improve. Note two things. The more you save, the more rapidly you will seem to be propelled towards achieving your financial goals. This is called the 'momentum principle'. It recognizes that it takes tremendous energy to overcome your initial inertia, and your understandable resistance to financial accumulation. However, once you start, it takes much less energy to continue.

Secondly, as soon as you start contemplating saving 10% of your income, a constellation of reasons why you can't possibly save will occur to you. You may be totally immersed in debt.

You may even be spending every dime that you earn just to keep afloat. If you find yourself in this situation, don't despair. Begin saving just 1% of your income in a special account. These small amounts will add up at a rate that will astound you. As you become comfortable with saving 1%, increase it to 2%, then 5%, and so on. Within a year, you will find yourself getting out of debt and saving 10%, and even 20% of your income without it really affecting your lifestyle.

16. *The Law of Magnetism*

The more money you save and accumulate, the more money you attract. This law has been the foundation of wealth building throughout human history. Money is a spirit. It goes where it is loved and respected. The more positive emotions you associate with your money; the more opportunities you will attract to acquire more.

Wealth consciousness attracts money the way a magnet rivets steel to itself. That is why it is vital for you to start accumulating money, no matter your situation, and no matter how small an amount. Energized by your faith, desire and hope, that money will begin to attract more to you faster than you can imagine. It takes money to make money.

Take time every week to reflect on your financial situation. Identify ways to creatively and intelligently deploy your finances. The more time you take to think intelligently about your finances, the better the decisions you will make and the more money you will have to think about. To compound your fortune, the more you think about your savings and investments, the more of them you will attract.

17. The Law of Accelerating Acceleration

The faster you move towards financial freedom, the faster it will move toward you. As you accumulate more money, more will move towards you from a variety of different places. Most millionaires literally work themselves to the bone before getting their first real break. However, after that, more and more opportunities flow to them from all directions.

18. The Law of Real Estate Business

The value of a piece of real estate is the future earning power of that property. To put it differently, the value of a piece of property is determined by the income that it can generate when it is developed to its highest and best use from now into the future.

Millions of acres of desert land have no real value, and no future earning power because they cannot be developed to generate income, or satisfy any human needs.

Vast swathes of some cities have declining property values because growth and development have come and gone and will probably not return. Every day, people are selling properties at far less than they paid for them, simply because these properties have declined in earning power, and therefore in value. In real estate, you make your money when you buy and you realize it when you sell. This a vital principle. It is only by purchasing property at the right price and under the right terms that you can sell it at a profit. The more carefully you investigate a property, and the more favorable your purchase offer, the more likely you are to obtain a deal that will enable you to later sell that property. The paramount key to real estate is location. Your ability to choose a piece of property in an excellent location is key to its earning power.

19. The Law of Internet Business

The technological utility of the Internet is focused on increasing the speed and reliability of the transmission of vital information. This is why the three keys to Internet success are Faster, Cheaper and Easier. People are in a hurry. Furthermore, everyone desires the lowest possible price to fulfil their needs, as easily as possible and with the greatest convenience possible. This is why the most successful Internet companies are those that offer products and services faster, cheaper and more easily than their competitors.

All three must exist for an Internet company to survive and thrive. In a nutshell, the value of an Internet company is directly proportional to the value of the information it provides.

The only real value of information is what people are willing to pay for it, and it is only by selling sufficient products and services at a profit that an Internet company can survive.

In summary, there are four keys to monetary success. First, earn as much as you possibly can by being one of the best in your field, such that you are paid extremely well for what you do.

Secondly, hold on to as much money as you possibly can, because it is not the amount you make, but the amount you keep that counts in the long run.

Thirdly, keep your cost of living on a leash. Look for every opportunity to be frugal and thrifty. Buy less expensive items. Most millionaires are very careful with their expenditure. This is how they became millionaires in the first place.

Finally, the key to monetary success is careful investment, and making your money grow as rapidly as possible. Due to the miracle of compound interest, you can become wealthy in just a few years by saving and investing 10% to 20% of your income every month.

This being a wonderful time of global economic growth, by applying these laws, you can fulfill your financial destiny and become wealthy.

CHAPTER 5

MULTIPLE STREAMS OF INCOME

The Millionaire and His Income

To become a millionaire in the truest financial sense of the word is to be aware that only multiple income streams will eventually lead to the long-term acquisition of the humongous sums of money, and the diversity of material assets, that situate one in the millionaire class. No authentic millionaire generates income from only one stream of income. However, it is equally pertinent to note that not all streams are suited to a one particular millionaire. To put it differently, to each person his own cup of tea.

In the present age, much noise is made about get-rich-quick schemes that are purportedly capable of making one a millionaire overnight.

Let us make one thing perfectly clear. There never has, and will never be an easy path to material fortune that does not violate the laws of nature. There is no such thing as a free lunch. Financial success will always have a price tag, and the components of this price, which include vision, creativity, proper planning and hard work, must be paid for upfront. The New Living Translation of the Bible clarifies that:

"Good planning and hard work lead to prosperity, but hasty shortcuts lead to poverty." (Proverbs 21:5)

Flash-in-the pan success is not sustainable. This is why the notion of 'overnight success' can, at best, be considered a faulty description of legitimate human achievement. To achieve anything worthwhile requires effort and effort takes time to expend. A prominent American who made his mark in the movie industry, once said, "Thirty years is one very long night!"

The truth is that most of us do not seem to possess an overwhelming, burning and all-consuming desire to earn a great deal more money than we require for sustenance at a comfortable level. In other words, most people have built a permanent nest in their financial comfort zone, and lack a desire to savor the glittering dividends that life offers.

What this amounts to is a refusal to trade one's time for money, or at the very least, reduce the amount of time one spends making good money.

The average millionaire was not born with the proverbial silver spoon in his mouth. Instead, he resolutely commits valuable time to earning money that can guarantee a healthy balance between the time he spends working and that doing all the other things he likes to do. Indeed, his money regenerates itself, even while he is asleep.

These are the typical income streams of most millionaires:

Earned Income

Earned income is the money that you earn by engaging in an activity in exchange for money. It is the salary you earn by working for someone else. This is where your quality of life will potentially suffer the most because you will be trading your time for money.

In most cases, jobs will pay you just enough to 'stay out of the broke zone'. The principal reason why most people are not able to think beyond earning a salary is because a job tends to provide a 'relatively' comfortable zone. This prevents them from leading an extraordinary life.

The ultimate result is that you spend the maximum amount of your time in this income stream, yet will receive only a minimum amount of money.

Profit Income

Profit income is money that you earn by selling something for more than it costs you, for example, in a business that sells goods at a profit, whether at the retail or wholesale level; as distributors or manufacturers. You need to be an entrepreneur to earn profit. You might need a huge investment, or you could start a small business for profit with a small investment. This will also require a huge investment in time, at least in the initial stages, and certainly until you learn to manage it well and it can run on its own steam.

"She considers a field and buys it; From her profits she plants a vineyard." (Proverbs 31:16)

Entrepreneurship involves risk taking. Most people who are salary earners find it difficult to make the move to become entrepreneurs because they lack the courage to take additional risks.

To become an entrepreneur who earns a profit, you will need to identify a product, or service to sell, and not only manage your sales well, but also your clients.

With profit income, the money you want is always in someone else's pocket. To get him to give you some of that money, you need to offer him a valuable product or service.

Interest Income

Interest income is the money you earn from lending your money for someone else's use, for example, depositing it in the bank, or lending it to the government in the form of Treasury Bills. This is a great source of passive income. Active involvement becomes unnecessary once the paperwork is done. Combined with the power of compound interest, and the fact that this is a passive stream with minimal risk, it can be a very profitable source of income generation.

Dividend Income

This form of income is even more attractive than interest income, because, not only is it equally passive, but it also makes you an equity holding shareholder of a company. This is the money you earn as a return on the share portfolio you own in a company.

Most companies announce dividend earnings on shares at the end of their financial year. If you invest wisely and in good blue chip companies, your dividend income could far exceed what you would earn from interest income, since you are also a party to the Capital Gains that the share price accumulates.

Rental Income

This is the money that you earn from renting out an asset, like a house, or a building. Although this can be a good source of income, there are inherent drawbacks. One of the biggest is the amount of money required to acquire or create an asset that can generate regular rental income. The other big drawback is the difficulty in liquefying such assets on short notice in times of desperate need, or when you need to move or re-balance your portfolio.

Capital Gains

This is the money you earn from an increase in the value of an asset that you own. For example, when you buy shares at $10 and sell them at $11, the $1 is capital gains, or if you bought your house for $200,000, and later sell it for $220,000, your capital gain is $20,000.

Royalty Income

This is the money you earn from allowing someone to use your products, ideas, or processes. They do all the hard work and make the revenue, and pay you a small percentage of whatever they earn. For instance, if you have a McDonald's Franchise, what you pay as compensation to McDonald's for using their processes, logo, and marketing is royalty income for them.

If you are a writer, you are paid a royalty for every copy of the book sold by your publisher. The biggest challenge is to create something unique and then make it replicable. You will need specialized skills to create such an asset, but once created, there is virtually no limit to the amount of money you can earn from it.

These are the seven principal sources of income of most millionaires. However, the average millionaire won't have all seven. In fact, most won't have more than two. Take billionaire Warren Buffet, who made the bulk of his fortune using Capital Gains and Dividend Income. He specialized in Capital Gains of companies on the stock market, while constantly honing his skills in valuing companies and investing in them.

Bill Gates generated humongous income through Profit Income and Royalty Income. He created a company, and used it to float an asset called 'Windows', a software tool that totally revolutionized the way we interact with computers. Gates has also invested enormous portions of his wealth in other sectors, like stocks and bonds.

In summary, you should focus on what you can do right now in one of these income streams, and then become the best player in a small niche in that income stream. However, note that the biggest risk to your financial life is being dependent on only one income stream.

CHAPTER 6

THE PRINCIPLES OF TIME MANAGEMENT

An Overview

Time is man's most precious commodity. Time already lost cannot be regained. The best one can do is resolve to make more effective use of the future. A future millionaire must learn how to achieve an effective finish to the day's work. Difficult as it seems, it is not a Herculean task to flawlessly complete the task at hand. However, we do need to be quite passionate about the task. The key word here is 'passion'. When we find a task unattractive, we tend to lack motivation to see it through. Indeed, the task may actually become repulsive to us. In the broad sense, the ability to manage time properly is a prerequisite for demonstrating how much we desire to achieve our set objectives.

What is needed is the right attitude. The ability to concentrate on the present moment is a requirement for engaging in tedious work. Most millionaires have a 'future orientation' that allows them to envisage their results before achieving them, and this enables them to savor the satisfaction that the completed task will bring. In truth, even the most boring activity can be performed if we expect positive consequences.

An Active Approach to Work

Future oriented people tend to cope well with difficult or tedious tasks. This is because of their propensity to adopt an active approach to their work that allows them to take control of their work, and not the other way around. When our work controls us, we tend be sluggish and lack enthusiasm and energy while doing it. That is why an active approach to tasks is a common denominator among most millionaires.

Embracing an active approach that avails him a clear view of the future, the average millionaire must master six skills to become a master of time management.

The Skills of a Master Time Manager

The first skill is communication. Poor or inadequate communication wastes time. For instance, if your employee does not understand your objectives, he may do the opposite of what you expect of him. We must dedicate sufficient time to ensuring that everyone understands our instructions and intentions. This will avoid misunderstandings, and minimize the chances of workflow disruption.

It is vital that we understand what others expect of us, and that they understand what we expect from them. High priority engagements demand written confirmation. For example, you should send an email to those that have been invited to an important meeting, asking that they confirm their attendance. On the other hand, if you are invited to a meeting, it behoves you to send an email confirming your attendance, at least a day prior to the meeting. As a rule of thumb, you must take responsibility for your communication. If the task you delegated was performed poorly, you are probably to blame for giving ambiguous instructions.

The second skill is discipline, and this is the most important characteristic of a master time manager. Discipline lies at the core of peak performance.

Being disciplined means that you always remember the most important tasks, and that, not only are you consistent in your daily, weekly, and monthly schedule, you never allow yourself to become distracted from your set goals. Discipline should not necessarily connote making your existence a living hell. It simply means that you have a routine that you are faithful to. You are never late. You always organize your tasks and complete them on time. You don't miss your daily exercise. You can use discipline to establish positive habits that cumulatively make your life much easier.

The third skill is a formidable memory. Contrary to popular belief that most people are afflicted with poor power of recall, the truth is that they merely have a poor approach. While we all fall prey to forgetfulness at times, our brain is wired to serve us with a good memory. All we need do is offer our memory a helping hand. Try to focus your attention on the most important things, and repeat them every once in a while if you notice that you have trouble remembering them.

Fortunately, this is the 21st century in which you do not have to remember everything. There are hundreds of apps to help you remember things. Master one such as a Google calendar.

The fourth skill is planning. Future oriented people are consummate planners. Planning ahead of time significantly increases your chances of success in any endeavor. You know where to go; what to do, and how to do it. However, there is a world of difference between having a plan and bringing it to fruition. A plan is not a guarantee of success. What's more, they tend to fail quite often. However, the activity of planning is of vital importance because it prepares us for action. Even if the situation is not proceeding as we conceived it, we are still prepared, and we know exactly what our goal is. Without planning, our chance of success remains dim, even if everything goes the best possible way.

In planning, we must take into consideration possible obstacles, and give ourselves the latitude of a number of options to choose from. If plan A doesn't work, we can switch to plan B, or C. We must remain as flexible as we can, so that no sudden eventuality will catch us off guard.

The fifth skill is checking. You should continually revise your processes as you proceed. Take periodic breaks to ensure that you haven't lost sight of your main goal. Pause to acknowledge completed tasks that are actually your small victories. Be humble enough to analyze your mistakes and learn from them. Assess your processes to ensure that your train of thought is still on the right track, and that you are still operating in line with your plan.

You may identify certain unnecessary activities that should be immediately eliminated from the original vision. These types of checks do not take much time, yet can save plenty of it.

The sixth skill is organization. Being organized may be the key factor for your success. It will not only save a lot of time, but much potential physical and mental stress. For instance, it is vitally important that your work environment is organized in such a way that you know exactly how to move about it in an effective and efficient manner. Refuse to spend your precious time searching for a pen, a piece of paper, your notes, or anything else that you need for your work. The same goes for your working device. Keep your PC clear. File all information in the right folders. This takes seconds while saving you hours of needless searching. Your policy should be, 'Everything in its place; a place for everything'.

Organize your office to be comfortable, and enriched with items that arouse positive emotions, like photos of your family. When you are organized, you don't have to worry about being late or getting overwhelmed with tasks, because you are always up to date with your activities. Furthermore, if your work place is neat, tidy and clear, you will feel much more comfortable spending time there.

Nine Principles of Time Management

Having dispensed with the foundational skills that one must possess to manage time more effectively, we turn to the core principles of time management.

Remember; you can't make up for lost time. You can only do better in future. For the average person, the time management dilemma includes struggling to find time during the daily hustle and bustle of life to embark on crucial personal projects, trying to juggle the demands of a 9-5 work schedule with the ambition of engaging in a personal business, or even the tendency to push crucial chores towards the weekend, and then onto the next week.

Time management is one of the most important skills that anyone aspiring to great wealth must have under their belt. While there is a plethora of information on this subject, certain basic strategies to manage time can be applied to every situation.

The following core principles of time management will not only help you lead a productive and balanced life, but also set you on the path to genuine and sustainable financial success.

- **Devote Time to Careful Planning**

Planning is of vital importance, no matter what you do. Take a few minutes in the morning to plan your activities for the day. For a hectic schedule, strive to reduce distractions to the barest minimum. You can also use various personal planning tools to plan and organize your schedule. These include calendars, wall charts, notebooks, pocket diaries, index cards and electronic planners. List all your tasks and schedules so that you can easily highlight your priorities.

It will serve you well to follow these guidelines as you use your planning tool:

* *Record all activities on your planning tool.*

* *Review your planning tool as your day proceeds.*

* *Always carry your planning tool with you.*

* *Make a list of your priorities on the tool and stick to it.*

* *If you are using an electronic planner, synchronize it with your PC.*

* *Ensure that you have a backup system for your planning tool.*

At the end of each workday, invest a few minutes in making a list of things you wish to accomplish the following day.

- **Organize and Prioritize**

Former President of the United States, Dwight D. Eisenhower, taught the world a valuable lesson in time management. He said that he had two kinds of problems: important and urgent, and that they are different. This principle became so valuable that an app named Priority Matrix, that allows for differentiation between 'Do Now' and 'Critical' tasks, was developed.

The most fundamental premise of effective time management is differentiating between what is important and what is urgent. Note that the most important tasks are not necessarily the most urgent ones and vice-versa. Most of us allow urgent tasks to dominate our lives. While both types of tasks can be done together, experts suggest that, one should first focus on important tasks regardless of their urgency.

Focusing on what you wish to accomplish will give you full control of your time. The easiest way to prioritize your tasks is to make a to-do list on daily, weekly or monthly basis, depending on your lifestyle.

Rank the items on your list on the basis of priority as high, medium and low. Execute and mark off the highest priorities first.

- **The 80/20 Rule**

This is known as the Pareto Principle. It recognizes that only 20% of your hard work produces 80% of your results. Therefore, the principle prescribes that you focus that 20% on making the most effective use of your time. Simply identify your most important tasks and follow these five steps:

  * *Mentally focus on your expected outcome.*

  * *Break that outcome down into the actions needed to execute the task.*

  * *Execute with total dedication, and as accurately as you can.*

  * *Identify and execute the next most important task.*

  * *Repeat until complete.*

- **Focus on One Task at a Time**

Most people try to do too much all at once and end up achieving virtually nothing.

People who try to accomplish multiple goals are usually less dedicated, and have fewer chances of succeeding, than those who fixate on a single goal at a time.

As much as possible, potential millionaires concentrate on one thing at a time. Present moment awareness is key to the success of most millionaires. Remain focused exclusively on whatever has your attention in the present moment. When you speak, speak. When you listen, listen. Be present in the moment so that you can fully concentrate on the task at hand. Practice doing one thing at a time and eventually it will become your normal routine.

- **Eliminate Distraction**

The following scenario is a common one: You are seated at your desk, determined to conclude a task at hand, no matter what. As you switch on your laptop, you notice a friend's message on Facebook, or a text message on your phone. Pronto! You abandon that important task. Distractions are inevitable, and can be near impossible to avoid. It can be particularly challenging to stay focused on a task for hours at a time. Practice the following strategies:

* *Put down your phone*: Constant unscheduled phone calls and messages are common distractions. You can check your calls and inbox every 2-3 hours.

* *Close Your Web Browser.* Engage your willpower and log off your social media profiles.

* *Wear Headphones.* If you work in a cubicle, wear noise-cancelling headsets to make the world a quiet and peaceful place.

* *Take a Break.* Take a short break if you feel distracted by something, or feel tired after working for long hours at a time. Short breaks will help you to relax, and clear your mind.

- **Delegate**

Delegation means identifying tasks that can be handled by others, and assigning them accordingly. This will free up time to devote to other core activities. Select appropriate persons who can assist you, and share your responsibilities in the best possible way. Such persons should have the appropriate skills, interest, experience and authority required to accomplish the task.

Be specific and clear while defining your tasks and expectations. Also allow such persons some latitude to personalize the assigned tasks. Occasionally check to ensure that the person is progressing in the right direction. Finally, reward the person for a job well done, or indicate respectfully that you will need to make improvements.

- **Maintain a Healthy and Stress-Free Lifestyle**

Caring for your body will help you rejuvenate mentally and physically. Only people with a healthy mind and body can accomplish their tasks swiftly, easily and efficiently.

Practice managing your time in synchrony with your biological clock by scheduling priority tasks for the peak time of the day, when your energy levels are at their highest. If you don't manage your time well, you will end up struggling with moodiness, fatigue and stress.

Engage in regular exercise. Each time you work out, you will feel much healthier and filled with renewed energy, ready to tackle all your tasks for the day.

- **Learn to Say "No"**

Unless something truly important comes up, practice saying 'no' to tasks that make you feel under pressure. Save your energy and concentration for the activities that are important to you, and which you enjoy.

Resolutely avoid getting too much on your plate and becoming overwhelmed with work. This does no one any good. Realize that it is perfectly in order to decline tasks that overwhelm you.

- **Make Realistic Schedules**

Plan your schedule before the week starts. Don't strive for perfection, as nobody is perfect. Rather, focus your efforts on being excellent and simply refuse to worry about things that you cannot control or handle. Stay positive. When you feel stressed, take a ten-minute break to do things that you enjoy. Take care of your health, eat and drink healthy, exercise daily, sleep well and laugh as much as you can.

In conclusion, whether you already manage your time properly, or you are about to embark on the effort, these principles will help you achieve your goals. Start with proper planning. Then move on to organize and prioritize your tasks according to your current situation.

Utilize the 80/20 rule to focus on what is most important to you. Schedule activities in a realistic manner, and learn to say "No" to those tasks that are of little or no value. Also, make sure that you do one thing at a time, avoid distractions, and keep yourself healthy and stress-free. Finally, know the difference between sincere commitment and mere interest.

CHAPTER 7

PRODUCER VERSUS CONSUMER

Producing Vs. Consuming

We are all consumers, but not all of us are producers. The distinction between the two has compelling relevance in the 21st century when levels of consumption have reached record levels. Indeed, never in the history of mankind has there been such a multiplicity of opportunities for unbridled consumption.

Life in the fast lane of Consumption Avenue is fast and easy. These days, you don't even have to step out of your house to consume food, music and movies. At the mere click of a button, you can have food delivered to your door. Your smart phone allows you to stream vast amounts of music, and download as many movies as you can watch.

Just about everything has become more readily available to the average person, including even education. The Internet has made it easier than ever to consume. The tragic truth is that we have strayed so far along the path of consumption that we have totally lost the wisdom to produce something of value. There should be a balance between consuming and producing. To put it succinctly, it is best to strive for an admixture of producing and consuming in your life, in which producing assumes greater prominence. It is so easy and convenient to consume. However, it's overall disadvantage is that, not only is it ultimately unfulfilling, its utility tends to decrease progressively the more you indulge yourself.

While consuming is incredibly easy and requires little or no effort, producing is the exact opposite. Producing something of worth, or of value, demands expenditure of effort, yet the results may not be immediately evident. To be a producer, you need to be determined, patient, exert your skills, and be able to think outside the box. Even though producing may appear quite unenjoyable, it is really what we, as human beings, are innately wired to do, and certainly, what also gives us the greatest satisfaction.

Our ancestors had to produce, or create, in order to survive and sustain themselves. In medieval times, you had to catch a fish, spear an antelope, or build a hut, or you would not last very long.

Simply put, our intrinsic value as human beings is based on what we can contribute to our communities, and the greater society. This does not imply that you have to be producing something of value for others all of the time in order to be considered valuable. Most certainly, you should also be producing something for your own benefit. However, to arrive at a place of considerable material fortune, you will have to produce much more than you consume.

What will you contribute? Will you start writing a blog? Will you create a piece of music? Will you invent something? Will you start a business? What human need will you fill? Why We Should Produce? Production reflects and validates our innate sense of purpose, and the desire to leave an imprint on the world, regardless of how small or big. We all derive a true sense of satisfaction from creating something out of nothing. Our ideas and thoughts, translated into concrete actions, can create a massive ripple effect that can change our lives, and our world, for the better.

The richest companies in the world; Amazon, Google, and Facebook, started out as simple ideas in the minds of their founders. These ideas were actualized through actions and deeds. A producer takes his thoughts and ideas, and turns them into something real. You can start out small by producing a poem, a painting, or a piece of music.

Once you successfully create these things, you can aim bigger and better, and produce a screenplay, a novel, a film, or a multi-million-dollar business. What skills and abilities do you currently possess? Make a list of your interests and hobbies.

Producing something of value demands hard work and effort. It will not be an instantaneous accomplishment, but may take months, and sometimes years, depending on the enormity and complexity of your project. Once you successfully launch your first product, you will start to appreciate the rare privilege of possessing the innovation and creativity to produce something original and unique. There is an innate sense of satisfaction in crafting something out of nothing.

Lasting happiness does not come from consuming the things of this world. Rather, it comes from bringing into the world things that weren't previously in existence. Depending on what you produce, you will also be making a positive contribution to the lives of others. It could be a business that will hire employees, or a bridge that will connect two towns. Furthermore, what you produce may even prove to be a legacy by lasting beyond your lifetime on Earth.

Offer yourself the golden opportunity to do more, write more, and build more. By being a producer, you create value for the world while building your own skills, abilities, and knowledge. Engage in a soul-searching exercise. Compile a list of your daily activities. Note the amount of time you spend on producing and consuming. Embark on the wholesome habit of producing more than you consume by resolutely devoting more hours to production time. The return on investment on time devoted to producing something far outweighs any benefits you could possibly get from consuming a video game, or a music album.

Start from scratch, if you must. Do your best to use your skills and abilities to produce something totally original. By no means are the books you've read, the movies you've watched, the music you've listened to, and the gourmet food you have eaten, inherently bad. However, you should invest some of the time you have spent consuming other people's products in creating your own product. Produce your own novel; your own play; your own symphony; your own business, or your own food recipe. These are all ways through which you can find fulfilment and meaning as a producer. Your lifetime will not last for eternity. You won't have forever to do both producing and consuming.

Ultimately, it may serve you better to choose producing over consuming, as you may find that you're not only good at it, but you like it much more than being a consumer.

Producers Spend on Investment; Consumers Spend on Distraction. Whereas most people spend most of their time consuming, the average millionaire typically becomes successful by being a producer. What's more, there is a clear distinction between the spending habits of a producer and a consumer that can ultimately shift the scale between success and failure in your financial life.

The difference between the way producers and consumers spend money is actually quite simple. Producers spend money on investment. Consumers spend money on distraction. Producers view their money as a resource to help them accomplish goals, and they spend it accordingly. They spend money on investment, and in ways that enable the money to work for them, even while they are asleep. Consumers, on the other hand, use their money as a resource that distracts them from their set goals, either consciously or subconsciously. Rarely do they spend money in ways that enable it to work for them. Consumers have a getting mindset with their money, while producers have a giving one.

Consumer Habits

Consumers generally indulge in various distractions, which normally means entertainment of some form or other. They spend money to forget about unsavory situations. Examples include unplanned vacations; buying gadgets and technology and the most comprehensive TV packages, shopping binges, gambling, drugs and alcohol. These are ominously effective distraction tools, and consumers flock to them.

Another route of dissipation is the ego trip where consumers devote time and energy to burnishing their image. They spend money on things that they think project them in a certain way. The stark reality, however, is that the purpose behind it all is their own discontent. They need to project an image, since if they can get somebody to believe it, then it may actually be true. Generally, consumers have a skewed vision of the concept of value. The only thing that has value to a consumer is something that massages his ego. Sadly, such items actually only have value for the seller; that is the producer, and not the buyer.

Producers' Habits

Producers, on the other hand, desire to spend money on just one thing; investment. Producers also understand that investments usually require time to mature. They do not subscribe to the notion of quick-fix schemes. The typical producer will usually engage in the following types of investment to attain his set goals:

1. *Financial Investment*: This involves spending money with the specific purpose of making money, and includes the purchase of stocks, bonds, real estate, or investment in a business. The sole purpose of this sort of spending is financial return.

2. *Self-Investment*: There are two main categories of self-investment:

• *Personal and Professional Development:* Books, classes, seminars, courses, personal coaching and mentoring, or anything that can help you to acquire the skills you need to achieve your goals.

• *Health and Wellness:* Producers realize that optimal health is a wise investment, and not an unbearable cost. To achieve this, they insist on good food and adequate nutritional supplements as well as regular exercise through a gym membership.

3. *Investment in others:* Producers easily recognize the value in investing in others. More often than not, such an investment is not intended for financial gain, but rather, a relationship gain, social gain, time gain, or quality gain. As they invest in themselves, they invest in others through the instrumentality of philanthropy and service. Their service tends to include paying for services from people who can offer better performance than them in some activity or another, in the process saving them valuable time. The expected return on investment is time or quality.

Producers understand that success requires a great team, even in a sole proprietorship. It also includes rewarding those that give them good service.

Do we, by any stretch of the imagination, allude that producers don't have fancy cars, beach houses, and the other finer things in life? We do not. Producers also purchase luxury items. The difference is that they spend the bulk of their resources on investments that yield them the dividends to spend on such luxuries.

Finally, proper resource utilization is a key skill for success. Money is simply one of your resources; very much like time, people and raw materials.

If you want to accomplish your life vision, and to be true to your purpose, you must spend most of your time on the producer side of the resource spectrum. In the final analysis, achieving a sustainable balance between producing and consuming is the ultimate elixir of success.

CHAPTER 8

THE PRINCIPLES OF BUSINESS LEADERSHIP

Vision

To be a visionary is to be a dreamer. Yet, there are two types of dreamers. There are those who vegetate on their dreams, refusing to translate them into reality. Conversely, there are those who understand and appreciate the creative mind of the divine. The latter are dreamers who take identifiable steps to fulfill their dreams. They insist on reshaping our world by creating something out of apparent nothing; re-creating our world for the better and creating untold wealth for themselves and for others in the process. These are the people who have vision. Indeed, it all starts with vision. Vision represents your ability to transform, in the present moment, into your future form. Vision is eloquent validation of your creative imagination.

It is undoubtedly the fundamental emotive force that drives all extraordinary achievement. If you were to attempt to identify the most potent motive for your actions, it would have to be vision.

Vision is the critical ability that allows you to see beyond your current reality. It lies behind your compelling necessity to create. Indeed, it is your innovative competence to invent what does not yet exist. It is vision that will allow you to arrive at the wisdom, that the quality of your life will be determined by the degree to which you do the right thing, for the right reason, in the right manner, and at the right time. It is those who have this sort of vision that have become emperors of their own mind.

Empires of the Mind

Make no mistake, the true millionaire is that individual whose mind account is bulkier than his bank account. We all know that it is easier to destroy than to build. We see a simple instance of this truth in the fact that it takes months to erect a magnificent mansion, yet it takes a bulldozer barely few hours to demolish it. By the same token, it takes years of hard work to amass a worthy and formidable fortune. But, with just one miscalculation, that fortune can come cascading down like a pack of cards, and a millionaire loses all his money, and his financial security.

This is why it is of vital importance for us to appreciate that, in very practical terms, the financial empires of the future will not be built on a mere material dimension. They will be built in the mind. In that future, which is so close that we must assume that it is here already, the true measure of wealth will be how much an individual is worth in his mind, especially in the devastating eventuality that he loses all his money. That is why the true millionaire is the man who invests more in his mind than his bank account.

Purpose

You were created to fulfill a unique purpose on Earth. God has manifested in you in physical form to fulfill a precise purpose. To put it differently, you have a unique gift or talent, and a unique way of expressing it. In other words, there is something that you are divinely equipped to do better that anyone else in the world. Even more interesting is that, for every unique talent, and unique expression of that talent, there are also unique human needs. That is why, in trying to identify your own definite purpose, you must do three things:

First, you must acknowledge the divinity within you.

The Bible says in John 10:34, *"Is it not written in your law, I have said you are gods?"*

Secondly, you must identify and express your unique talent.

When you have identified this, you must go further to identify the unique ways in which you express it. This means that there is one thing you can do, and one special way of doing it, that is better than anyone else.

Finally, the expression of your unique talent must meet a specific human need.

You must use your talents to consciously match the needs of your fellow human beings. That is when you will know real joy, and the true meaning of success. As it says in 1 Peter 4:10,

"Each one should use whatever gift he has received to serve others, faithfully administering God's grace in its various forms."

Passion

Nothing worthwhile was ever achieved without passion. Take a look around you, and you will discover that really successful people are ruled by passion.

The only reason why they are so happy and successful is because they are pursuing a calling for which they have deep passion. What exactly is passion? Passion is an intense emotional excitement about what one is doing. What is the work that gives you the greatest joy when you are doing it? This is a very important question. Anyone who does not have his passion at the tip of his tongue does not know his passion.

Most millionaires can articulate their passion in a split second. What will the world remember you for? What will be your legacy to mankind? What will make you stand out from the motley crowd, and be an outstanding person?

Originality

Strive to be an original. Always remember that genuine success is the reward you will receive in exchange for the service you render using your talents. If you give the best service, you will receive a commensurate reward.

Give yourself over completely to your gift, and your gift will give back to you abundantly. The best way to offer the best possible service is to give that service in such a refreshingly unique and original manner that you will always remain sought after to render that service any time it is needed.

Even better, you will always be referred to others who require the same service. You are on the way to your millions.

Integrity

In the book of Jeremiah; chapter 17:11, the Bible says,

"Like a partridge that hatches eggs it did not lay is the man who gains riches by unjust means. When his life is half gone, they will desert him, and in the end he will prove to be a fool."

Integrity simply connotes moral excellence. Living a life of integrity necessarily makes you a man of excellence. In all your dealings with others, insist on seeing people as an extension of God. Place a divine value on them by looking at them through the eyes of God.

Make no mistake about one indubitable fact. It is impossible to strike a cheap bargain with God's prosperity. All intelligent work must be backed by moral energy. Can a bubble last forever? No! Lack of integrity, like a bubble, will eventually burst. In your quest for wealth, you must commit to offer a just and equitable return for all that you receive. Action and reaction are equal.

The Golden Rule as stated by our Lord in the Book of *Matthew, chapter 7:12,*
"Do unto others what you would have them do to you"

simply cannot be circumvented. A man's fraudulent efforts are destructive and not constructive. Therefore, such a man does nothing but destroy himself.

The popular, yet patently dubious refrain is that no one can be completely honest in business. That statement is a false representation of the world of business. What it reflects is the condition of the speaker, being himself, in all probability, a dishonest and morally bankrupt person. All dishonest men think all men are dishonest. Conversely, all men of integrity think all men can be trusted, and so they treat all men with confidence, trusting them, and they are trusted in return.

Good will always triumph over evil and the upright man will always put the evil man to shame. Even brilliance will have to take its place behind integrity, for while a brilliant man may be quite unhappy and unfulfilled, nothing can rob the man of integrity of his state of permanent satisfaction.

The man of integrity is a great man indeed, and material fortune will come to him for four good reasons:

One, he easily wins the confidence of other people. Two, having reposed this confidence in him, they trust him.

Three, since he never violates this trust, he has a good reputation, and

Four, news of his good reputation spreads far and wide,

such that everyone wishes to do business with him, and of course, with this comes material affluence.

Courage

Seek the fortitude to accept that which you can do nothing about. Seek the discipline to act upon that which you can do something about. Seek the wisdom to know the difference between the two. Life is a school. At the University of Life, examinations take the form of everyday situations, some of which may not be particularly pleasant. Sadly, most of us are unable to accept the reality of such situations, many of which are to be expected in a business career. What is the reason for this? The most common one is a lack of courage, which is why a lot of people are prostrated with fear, unable to take a calculated business risk.

That is also what is responsible for most people's failure to accept and confront those challenges that may necessitate movement out of their comfort zone. This is the manifestation of fear of the unknown.

Courage is not the absence of fear, but mastery of fear. Fear that buries the talents of many people, preventing them from attaining their true potential. Fear and faith are polar opposites, because, on a fundamental level, what each of them brings to our lives are also opposites; with fear leading to failure, and faith leading to conquest. Your greatest challenge will be conquering fear and a corresponding development of courage, and since anything you practice over and over again eventually becomes a habit, you can only develop courage by acting courageously any time it is called for. A courageous person goes forward in spite of his fear.

Compassion

Compassion takes one above a self-centred existence, enabling one to reside in the heart of another person, and to think and feel with him. One is able to place oneself in the place of others, and be as they are. Compassion does not ask a wounded person how he feels. Rather, compassion becomes the wounded person.

Compassion seeks expression in the divine, as stated clearly in Psalms chapter 145:9,

"The Lord is good to all; He has compassion on all He has made."

Even in common-place business dealings, compassion should assume pride of place. People will always gravitate towards those businessmen who are amiable and kind, preferring to deal with them rather than with those who are hard and mean in disposition.

Lack of compassion finds expression in harshness, inflexibility and cruelty. Many fail in business because of a harsh disposition, and a cold demeanor that brooks no compassion whatsoever. This isolates one from those one has to deal with in business, be they employees or customers, gradually leading to the loss of money. Some businessmen labor under the illusion that diligence in business is not compatible with self-sacrifice. That is quite untrue.

The gains of selfishness are small but short lived, while the blessings of compassion are great and long-lasting. The beauty of compassion is such that its depth of understanding ensures that, while the unkind man sees only a man's clothes, the compassionate man sees the man and is not concerned with his clothes.

Perseverance

Patience is the ability to endure delay and hardship. To persevere, however, is to continue steadfastly, or in a determined manner. The proof of the love you have for your business is perseverance. If you passionately love what you do, every associated experience, whether pleasant or not, will be a source of learning, and nothing will seem like failure to you.

It is those who persevere and pass the test of endurance that are rewarded with success at the end of the day. Every failure brings you closer to your goal. Your failures are the price you pay for your future success.

Great people hardly use the word failure in self-reference. Why should they? After all, they know that there's no shame in making mistakes. What is unforgivable is refusal to learn from those mistakes. When you experience failure, accept it patiently because each failure is merely a stepping stone to your future vista of success.

Discipline

I will tell you a little story. An ancient army set out to conquer an empire, only to become lazy and complacent after invading the first village. While the soldiers were revelling in their captured loot of rich food, wine and women, a more diligent general overtook them to conquer the rest of the empire. This only happened because the army lacked discipline. And because they lacked discipline, they also lost focus. You must be disciplined.

True discipline is an indication of strength of character, since the stronger your character, the more you are able to side line life's distractions, and focus exclusively on the task at hand. Discipline connotes the willingness to do what needs to be done, when it needs to be done, whether or not it's convenient. Even if you master all the other attributes required for you to succeed, and you lack discipline, you won't get very far. Know one thing about great people. Whenever they are inspired to pursue a big objective, great purpose, which comes out of great discipline, arises in them.

Hard Work

If you have all the above attributes, and you refuse to apply yourself to hard work, your efforts will be in vain. Talent is a very common commodity. Everyone has it. What separates the talented person from the successful one is a lot of hard work.

The Chinese say that the journey of a thousand miles starts with the first step. This is very true. Anything you wish to achieve remains just that until you decide to act, and take steps to realize your objective. Hard and purposeful work is an important part of the journey called success. Struggle and progress are two wheels of the same cart. They are mutually involved in your gradual march to success.

Hard work pays. Life will never be a bed of roses. From the day you were born, you became part of a generation of people who have to toil hard to make meaning of their existence on earth.

There is no gain without pain. We have to embrace the pain. Seeking out and embracing it will make you better, stronger, faster, and more successful. Shying away from pain and seeking comfort will only make you weaker and unsuccessful.

If you choose to lay in bed all day, it is inevitable that progress will elude you. However, if you get up and take action, you will make progress. There is no such thing as overnight success.

CHAPTER 9

GIVING BACK

To Whom Much Is Given; Much Is Expected

The subject of giving has been preached so often that many people have stopped listening. However, you cannot aspire to be a millionaire without the giving mindset.

Christians should be the wealthiest people in the world. Unfortunately, they are not. We know that more than 90% of the Christians in the world are dead broke. Yet, to be rich is a choice, and to be poor is also a choice.

The fundamental root of Christian poverty may have more to do with a lack of true spiritual maturity than anything else. Spiritually mature people do not give themselves credit for their financial success, and their lives do not revolve around the pursuit of money for its own sake.

They are always conscious of the fact that, in allowing them to make money, God wants them to use His blessings for His glory.

One of the reasons why I decided to write this book is that much of the toxic teaching about wealth is the result of spiritual immaturity. Christians have been so constantly bombarded with the "money is evil" message that they have developed a guilt complex about accumulating money, even from worthy pursuits. If money were that evil, why would God's Word contain so many examples of faithful men and women who acquired massive wealth, yet remained totally devoted to God? Abraham, Isaac, Jacob, Joseph, Job, David, Solomon, Joseph of Arimathea, and Lydia are just a few examples of biblical heroes who honored God with the wealth He gave them.

Giving is God's nature and since we are clothed with His nature, we have no option but to become givers. It is human inclination to give to others in need.

For you to stand vindicated in the truth that God materially blesses as He deems fit, and that He blesses us so that we can be a source of blessing to others, and to validate the truth in the oft-quoted saying,

"To whom much is given, much is expected," (Luke 12:48)

you have to start giving back. You have to give back to your community, and to the field of endeavor that is the source of your wealth.

This is a Spiritual Law, and just like man-made laws, the Law of Giving Back should not be broken by a true Christian millionaire. You have to give in order to receive. You can choose where and how you give, but you must give in order to grow your seeds.

Seeds

Spare a moment to think about seeds. If you simply drop many seeds on the ground and forget about them, some may sprout of their own accord without receiving any attention from you. However, wouldn't many more sprout bountifully if they were properly attended to in the form of water and nutrients? That way, you would reap a bountiful harvest. Yes, if you put a 'little something extra' into your habit of giving, you truly would not be able to contain the bounty that would fill your cupboards.

You Can Never Out give God

You can give in any of many ways. However, one thing I can say with certainty is that you simply cannot out give God. A fundamental principle that we all need to be familiar with at the start of our careers is that the very thing that we are lacking in life is the one that we need to give more of. If it is money you need more of, give more of it to those in need of it. If your wardrobe is outdated, give the outdated clothes to those in need of clothing, and create a vacuum that God can fill with newer clothes.

From a business perspective, giving back helps to consolidate and solidify your standing in the community. One is truly baffled by people who point their finger at others for not giving back to their community. One's only response should be, "Why don't you give back yourself?" You could liken the situation to me becoming upset because my neighbor won't feed my kids while I feast alone every night in their presence. As the saying goes, charity begins at home.

Giving can be tremendously rewarding. You don't have to give away the shirt on your back, although that is not the worst thing you could do should a dire need for that arise. Sometimes, just doing a little something is worth the effort. It may make all the difference in the life of a child or a family in need.

I seldom, if ever, use phrases like 'Underprivileged people,' or 'Downtrodden people'. I don't use such phrases because none of God's creations is underprivileged, and we all have been in need of something or the other at some point in life. Just do a little something.

I have been so inspired by what I've seen some people do, while I have simply despaired at how little others do. A whole lot may not be necessary as the collective 'little somethings' add up to 'very big things'.

Social Responsibility

Our responsibility to society has become so imperative that, over the past few decades, the term "Social Responsibility" has assumed a prominent place in the lexicon of 'giving back'. Social responsibility is formally acknowledged as an ethical framework that encourages an entity, be it an organization, or an individual, to consider itself under obligation to act for the benefit of society at large.

Essentially, social responsibility has become a duty that every individual has to perform so as to maintain a balance between the economy and the ecosystems. Let us consider a few ways in which we can give back to society, while growing our businesses and material fortunes.

Local Sponsorships

Your business and yourself can support and sponsor just about anything that is of sustainable benefit to society. Sponsorships can be as big as supporting an entire school expansion program.

You can still take advantage of smaller sponsorship opportunities in your area; from sports teams to theatre clubs and youth choirs. Such local groups are often in desperate need of assistance to cover some of their costs. These may even be in exchange for corporate adverts, so that your business can get a little extra exposure, while such local programs get the support they need.

Being a Part of the Community

Giving back to the community doesn't have to be predicated on money. You can also give back by committing your time, energy and involvement to communal causes. You can get involved in the community by identifying pre-existing charity drives that need your services or could use your facilities. You could also take the initiative to launch your own community events that enrich the local community.

How you get involved will depend on the type of business you run. An accounting firm, for example, could offer a money management workshop for retirees, or college students.

Think about initiatives that will benefit your community. Assess your services and resources to determine how and where you can step in and help.

Employee Involvement

Make volunteer work part of your company culture. Close the office for one day every three months and involve your employees in some volunteer initiative or another. Your employees could sign up to mentor high school students or volunteer for road marshal duties. There are many options for getting your employees involved in a cause, and all of them will help your business to give back.

Set Aside Part of Your Profits

If you want your business to make an even greater impact, incorporate giving back directly into your business model by donating a portion of your profits to a cause you care about.

Consumers who purchase your products will know that a portion of the money they pay will go towards supporting a charitable organization. This portion may be as small as 2%.

This might not seem like much, but as anyone involved in charitable work knows, every bit makes a difference. If you're interested in finding ways to give back within your business model, start small or think local. You will end up making a significant difference for your customers, your employees, your community and possibly even your sales.

The Giving Pledge

Important as money is to our sustenance, we need to shift our focus to something more enduring. Maybe one thing that is missing from the lives of most people is a genuine life mission. We need a legacy more impactful than just making money. It does not matter how long we stay on Earth; how much money we gather or how much adulation we receive. It is the amount of 'positive vibration' we radiate in life that matters.

Pursuing a great mission, and making a difference, can help us to do something other than just accumulate money. Giving back, and massively, out of what God has blessed us with can make a difference.

The Mysterious Path to Prosperity

An interesting angle to giving is that, the act of giving has no match when it comes to its sheer capacity to generate more of what it gives.

Anytime you give, with love, you unwittingly engage the universe in a symphony of economic advancement and monetary plenitude.

Although few people can unravel the mystery of the plenitude that accompanies generosity, it is widely acknowledged that to give is to be at the receiving end of more of what was given away. The act of giving is a very potent spiritual activity. It validates the essence of compassion as one of our Creator's motives, and His vehicle for the display of love. Every act of giving should be an act of love. That is why the act of giving is backed by tremendous spiritual energy.

Silent Giving

The most powerful form of giving is the one that is done silently. A perfect example is provided by the incredible story of the concealed magnanimity of one of the world's most reclusive billionaires; a man known by the nickname, 'The James Bond of Philanthropy'. His name is Charles Francis "Chuck" Feeney. He made his fortune as a co-founder of the Duty-Free Shoppers (DFS) Group, which pioneered the concept of duty-free shopping at the world's major airports.

Feeney gave away his fortune in secret for many years, until a business dispute resulted in the revelation of his identity in 1997.

Over the course of his remarkable life, Feeney has given away more than $8 billion. After secretly transferring his entire 38.75% stake in DFS, then worth about $500 million, to a foundation he kept concealed from even his partners, for years, through that foundation, he gave away money in secret, strictly instructing and requiring recipients not to reveal his identity. He gave his alma mater, Cornell University, $1 billion and donated $1 billion towards education in Ireland. In February 2011, Feeney became a signatory to The Giving Pledge founded by Bill Gates and Warren Buffet. Finally, in late 2016, he gave away his last $7 million to the same recipient of his first charitable donation; Cornell University.

Although, as it says in Matthew 6:3,

"But when you give to the needy, do not let your left hand know what your right hand is doing,"

you are under no obligation to give anonymously. Let us assume that you are a philanthropist and you have just donated a million dollars to a worthy and notable humanitarian cause. If you did your giving in total anonymity, perhaps even going to the lengths, like Mr. Chuck Feeney, to conceal your identity as the giver, one might conclude that you gave without expectation of applause. On the other hand, you might choose to give the money at a publicized media event. The choice is yours. What is important is that you gave out of what you were blessed with.

Start Giving Today

You don't have to be a millionaire before you start giving. Start practicing how to give as a millionaire today. You won't regret it. If you find yourself challenged at first, start small. Embark on a back-to-school drive. Place a donation box in your office. Put a donate button on your website and give the proceeds to something you believe in. People will always need help. You can help more than you can ever imagine. God loves a cheerful giver. Just give, and watch your harvest start coming in. Challenge yourself to give for the next six months. Document what you do and look at your life a year from now. Don't be surprised if you see a remarkable change in your fortunes. Simply give, and keep on giving.

CONCLUSION

We have come to the end of our joint excursion into the world of the millionaire, our principal objective having been to identify the enduring rules of wealth acquisition that the very wealthy have always subscribed to, even as far back as the days of King Solomon. If you don't believe you can be a millionaire, you can never become one. It all begins in the mind. As a man thinks in his heart, so is he. All things are created twice; first in the spiritual realm, and then on the physical plane. You have to become a millionaire on the mental level before the physical manifestation of your prosperity can make itself evident.

Many myths surround millionaires. That is hardly surprising. The subject of wealth is a very fascinating one. However, you need to be very careful about how seriously you take such myths to heart, because believing them can easily become one of the biggest hurdles on your way to becoming a millionaire. Believing the myths about wealth and the wealthy can prevent you from becoming wealthy yourself. Furthermore, saying, "I can't", or "It's not possible for someone like me to become a member of the millionaire class" can easily turn into a self-fulfilling prophecy. Carefully police your self-dialogue so that you don't end up short-changing yourself by truncating your beautiful potential.

A lot of self-defeated people believe that the wealthy do not really earn their money through honest means, take unreasonable risks with their money, and tend to have an edge over others by having a privileged education and careers. However, the popular belief that most millionaires inherited their money has been found to be false. In fact, most millionaires are first-generation rich; meaning that they worked hard, made sacrifices, and coasted to financial success on a viable plan.

Some people view wealth the way lightning strikes. For such people, there is no human control over when and where 'the millionaire lightning' will strike next. On the contrary, luck does not play such a prominent role in wealth acquisition. Most millionaires exerted hard work, discipline, resilience and perseverance to build their wealth from the ground up.

It is also not true that the average millionaire is a reckless risk-taker. Most understand that risk is something to be managed, not avoided.

They tend to tread carefully, weighing and counterbalancing the risk and potential reward, and then move forward cautiously and confidently, in full realization that their success is in their own hands. In truth, most millionaires do not take stupid risks just to rapidly build wealth. Most tread the slow and steady path to fortune, many taking decades to attain millionaire status. Believe it or not, more than half of the world's authentic millionaires did not become millionaires until they were almost 50. They tend to balance risk and reward with a long-term mind-set.

Ultimately, however, one must have a higher purpose for accumulating money, rather than simply amassing a fortune for its own sake. For the truly spiritual millionaire, the real reason for amassing a colossal fortune may not be that money matters to them so much. In fact, such people may not even see the gratification of their material needs as an end unto itself. For some, it may simply be a way to show others that, with faith, they are capable of achieving just about anything they set their minds to.

There is one fact that we can never run away from. One of our greatest possessions while we exist on this earthly plane is freedom, and wealth can give us freedom. Naturally, we all aspire to freedom, for with it, many an illusion we labor under will vanish into thin air.

Yet, despite the security that immense wealth gives them, many millionaires tend to finally arrive at the sublime understanding that true freedom is found in detachment, for it is only when we detach from our earthly wealth that we can truly attend to the supreme will of God.

In the final analysis, I humbly urge you, whether you have plenty of money, or just a little, to always maintain the appropriate equilibrium where money is concerned. Remember that money can be a faithful servant, but it can also quite easily become a tyrannical master. Always keep at the back of your mind that you did not bring money with you at birth, nor will you take it away with you when the Father calls you home. Always see money for what it is and no more. Enjoy your money, but refuse to let it take over your life. Shalom.

www.ingramcontent.com/pod-product-compliance
Lightning Source LLC
Chambersburg PA
CBHW030336100526
44592CB00010B/712